Predator Proof

Jo Saint

Copyright © Jo Saint, 2025

ISBN 978-1-915962-98-0
First published 2025 by Compass-Publishing UK

Edited and typeset by The Book Refinery
www.TheBookRefinery.com

Cover designed by © Alexa Whitten

The right of Jo Saint to be identified as the author of this work
has been asserted in accordance with the Copyright, Designs
and Patents Act, 1988.

All rights reserved. No part of this publication may be reproduced, stored in
a retrieval system, or transmitted, in any form or by any means (electronic,
mechanical, photocopying, recording or otherwise), without the prior
written permission of the publisher.

Content warning!
This book deals with sensitive matter and references to sexual assault.

*For every woman who may need this book.
This one is truly for you.
Stay safe.*

Contents

Preface	7
Prologue	9
Chapter 1 - Lessons from My Father	13
Chapter 2 - Situational Awareness:	17
Chapter 3 - Body Language	31
Chapter 4 - Am I Being Followed?	37
Chapter 5 - The Unwritten Contract	41
Chapter 6 - Environmental Conditions	45
Chapter 7 - Fight or Flight	49
Chapter 8 - Training for Survival	53
Chapter 9 - What to Carry for Protection	59
Chapter 10 - Recognising Your Most Vulnerable Moments	63
Chapter 11 - Report It! Report It! Report It!	67
Chapter 12 - Keep an Eye on Each Other	71
Chapter 13 - What Can Men Do to Make Women Feel Safer?	75
Conclusion	79
Poem: Between the Cracks (Content Warning)	82
References	85
Acknowledgements	90
About the Author	92

Keeping-safe tips

Trust your instincts.

Preface

I never imagined I'd write a book like this.

Not only did my police training teach me how to read situations and stay alert but so did my father. From an early age, he passed down invaluable lessons about awareness, trust and self-protection, which stuck with me long before I ever wore a uniform. Those lessons became part of who I am, and over time, they've taken on an even deeper meaning.

As a former police officer, I've spent years working in environments in which vigilance and safety were part of daily life. But even with all that experience, I've still walked home with my keys between my fingers. I've still changed my route at the last minute. I've still felt that unmistakeable gut feeling that something wasn't quite right.

And I know I'm not alone. Over the years, I've had countless conversations with friends, colleagues and women from all walks of life, and it's become clear that *we all feel it*. That quiet alertness. That flicker of discomfort. That instinct that tells you something might be off, even if you can't explain why.

This guide was born out of those shared experiences, that deep knowing and a desire to help. It's not here to alarm you or tell you how to live your life; it's here to offer real, practical advice you can use whether you're heading home, on a night out or simply navigating the world with a little more awareness.

I've also included a chapter for men on how they can help women, because many want to but aren't always sure how. This is for them too.

Thank you for picking this book up. I hope it gives you clarity, confidence and maybe even a little comfort.

Stay safe,

Jo Saint

Prologue

The scale of the crisis

In the UK, violence against women isn't just a crisis; it's an epidemic. The numbers are staggering, and the reality is devastating. In the year ending March 2022, an estimated *798,000 women* aged 16 and over experienced sexual assault, including attempts.[1] In addition, *70,600 rapes* were recorded by the police in England and Wales in the year ending March 2023.[2] These figures are only estimates as many more cases go unreported – buried under fear, shame and a system that often fails the survivors.

One way to grasp the magnitude of these crimes is by looking at the size of London's iconic double-decker buses. A standard London double-decker bus, such as the New Routemaster commonly used in London, can carry around 87 passengers in total – 62 seated (including wheelchair spaces) and up to 25 standing.[3] The number of women sexually assaulted in the UK each year could fill over 9,100 full double-decker buses. Each and every day, approximately 25 fully packed buses' worth of women experience this violation of their rights and safety, yet only about four buses' worth of victims report their assault – the

Crime Survey for England and Wales has found only around 16% of victims report the crime.[4]

To put this into even greater perspective, consider how long it would take to fill this year's worth of buses if they were lined up. This line would stretch around 100 kilometres, which is roughly the distance from London to Northampton (each of our standard London double-decker buses is approximately 11 metres long[5]). Yet despite the overwhelming scale of these crimes, only a small fraction of cases ever get reported.

While men also experience sexual violence, the numbers tell a starkly different story. Only *0.8% of men* reported experiencing sexual assault last year, compared to *3.4% of women.*[6] In the year prior to March 2022, *over 90% of adult rape victims knew the perpetrator*; specifically, 44% identified the perpetrator as a partner or ex-partner, 27% as another known individual (e.g. a friend or acquaintance), and 20% as a family member.[7]

Why this book matters

This book isn't about blaming men. It's about facing the reality that, as women, we must alter the way we navigate the world for our own safety. I've personally experienced this in my own city: changing my route home, adjusting my travel habits and making decisions based on safety rather than convenience.

Many women – me included on some days – often think, *Why should I have to? Men should be the ones taught not to assault women.* Although that's true, the statistics show we must still take responsibility for our own safety because no one else will or can do it for us.

PROLOGUE – THE SCALE OF THE PROBLEM

If you're an adult woman or even a teenage girl stepping into independence, you must take ownership of your security. We shouldn't have to live like this, but until systemic change happens, we must remain *alert, aware* and *prepared.*

What I'm about to share with you isn't just theoretical. These are insights and lessons passed down from my father and (as I'm a former police officer) law enforcement professionals, plus from my own experiences – including the times I got things hopelessly wrong.

The following chapters will outline both general and specific safety techniques for women in the UK. Whether they're at home, on public transport, in crowded city streets or in the quiet of their own neighbourhoods, women deserve to feel and be safe.

We'll explore how to navigate interactions with strangers, from avoiding dangerous situations to responding effectively if things go wrong. But perhaps even more crucially, we'll address the threats that come from closer to home – including how to recognise warning signs, set boundaries and take action against those who seek to harm us.

Safety isn't solely about physical techniques or self-defence (although that's very important); it's about knowledge, awareness and preparation. This book aims to equip you with the tools you need to move through the world with greater confidence and security – because *no woman should ever have to wonder if she'll become another statistic.*

Keeping-safe tips

We must still take responsibility for our own safety because no one else will or can do it for us.

CHAPTER 1

Lessons from My Father

It was cold and dark; the kind of evening that made me want to stay inside. But I had no choice – I had to walk to the shops with my dad to pick up the shopping. I lived in Enderby, Leicestershire, which was then a small rural village with a population of around 5,000 people (in 1991),[8] spread across 4.5 square kilometres.[9] While there were plenty of open green spaces, our home was on a newer estate about a 10-minute walk from the nearest shop: Kwik Save.

I always dreaded those walks. They felt like a chore, especially knowing I'd have to carry heavy shopping bags back, and going with my dad meant one thing: overpacked bags and a speed walk. Unlike my mum, who kept things light, he would fill them to the brim without a second thought. Still, there was no way out. We were off.

I think I was around 10 at the time. I remember walking up the road, struggling to keep up with my dad's ever-expanding strides, when he suddenly said: "Don't look around, but how many people are walking behind us?"

My mind froze as I processed his question. Careful not to cheat, I did exactly as he said. A few moments passed, but I had no idea. I strained my ears, trying to pick up footsteps, but the wind howled around me, rattling in my ears and drowning out any sound.

"What can you smell?" my dad prompted.

"Fags. I can smell cigarettes." *Ahh*, I thought, *I've got it.*

"What else?"

"Aftershave." I wasn't completely sure, but I thought I caught a hint of trendy cologne drifting on the breeze.

"What else?"

What else? I thought I'd done so well already, but my dad wanted more. What had I missed? Not wanting to lose this game, I stole a quick glance behind me. I spotted a few people walking.

My dad caught me. "Are you right?"

"Well, sort of... there are more people, though."

"That's right. Now listen – can you hear the jingling keys?"

He hadn't turned around, yet he'd noticed more than I had. As soon as he pointed it out, I heard them too.

"Yes," I said, pleased with myself once more.

"So, Jo, you can hear jingling keys. It's probably a man. Women don't usually wear keys on a chain; they keep them in their bags. Also, the aftershave – is it a young man's scent or something worn by someone older? The footsteps – are they heavy or light? Do you hear the click of heels or the sound of flat shoes?"

And so it continued. Every time we walked at night, it became a game, with me learning to see through my senses and to notice the world without looking directly at it. My dad was teaching me situational awareness and preparedness. He spoke about the dangers that men can pose to young girls and women, and how this skill – paying attention to the details others miss – was one of my first steps toward keeping safe.

Keeping-safe tips

If you think you're being followed, one simple trick is to stop abruptly and pretend to check your phone as if you've forgotten something.

CHAPTER 2

Situational Awareness:
The Power of Perception

Situational awareness is about being alert – not only to what's happening around you but also to what *isn't* happening. Sometimes, it's not the presence of something unusual that signals danger, but rather the absence of the usual: the sudden quiet on a busy street, the lack of eye contact from someone acting suspiciously or an instinctual feeling that something just isn't right.

The first step to being aware is making sure you're in a fit state to notice. I can't count the number of times I've seen women walking through the city, day or night, with their heads buried in their phones and earphones blocking out the world. That's two of your six senses (yes, six) switched off completely.

Your most relied-on sense is sight, yet if you're glued to your screen, you're missing potential dangers unfolding around you. Put your phone away. Take your earphones out of your ears.

Look up.

Pay attention.

Your safety starts with awareness.

Sight

All the time, we see things that we don't process. Our brains don't process everything equally. Instead, they selectively filter information and prioritise what we deem important while ignoring the rest. This phenomenon explains why we suddenly start noticing something we never paid attention to before, such as seeing our own car model everywhere after purchasing it. Understanding how we notice things – and what we overlook – can significantly improve our situational awareness.

The human brain is an incredible processing machine, which handles 80% of all sensory input through vision, but it doesn't absorb everything equally; instead, it relies on filters to sort through the overwhelming amount of data entering our eyes every second.[10]

Here are some key facts about our visual perception:

- We can process an image in as little as 13 milliseconds.[11]
- We remember 80% of what we see, compared to only 10% of what we hear and 20% of what we read.[12]
- Our peripheral vision covers approximately 120–140 degrees, but only 30 degrees are in clear focus; the rest relies on subconscious pattern recognition.[13] The more we notice, the more we recognise.
- Moving objects or high-contrast colours are twice as likely to be noticed than static or neutral-coloured ones.[14]

Why we notice familiar things more often

A well-known cognitive bias, the Baader–Meinhof phenomenon (also called the 'frequency illusion'[15]), explains why we suddenly start seeing something everywhere after it becomes relevant to us.[16] This happens because of the reticular activating system (RAS), which is a network in the brainstem that's responsible for filtering important versus irrelevant information.[17]

For example, before buying a car, we rarely notice that specific model on the road. However, after purchasing one, it feels like that model is suddenly everywhere. In reality, the number of those cars hasn't changed; our brain has simply decided it's now important. Studies in cognitive psychology show that individuals are significantly more likely to notice stimuli that are personally relevant or emotionally salient. For instance, one study using the emotional Stroop task – which examines the time participants take to name the colours of words they're presented with – found that participants took *20–30% longer to name the colour of emotionally charged words*, indicating that such words captured more of their attention.[18]

This selective attention doesn't just apply to words or objects such as cars; it affects how we perceive people, threats and opportunities in our environment. Imagine if you trained your mind to prioritise certain safety cues or behaviours; your brain's natural bias toward relevant stimuli could help you detect those threats more quickly and accurately, which would give you a meaningful advantage in terms of situational awareness and personal safety.

The art of noticing

Our brains are incredibly efficient at filtering information, but this comes at a cost: we're prone to what's known as 'change blindness', which is the failure to notice even major changes in a scene. Studies suggest that 40–50% of people fail to detect significant alterations in their surroundings, such as a car changing colour or objects disappearing.[19] This phenomenon becomes particularly dangerous in high-stakes environments where quick reactions are essential.

For example, imagine walking alone through a quiet street at night. You pass a parked car with someone sitting inside it, but your mind dismisses it as unimportant. A few moments later, you hear footsteps behind you, but your brain doesn't register that they could belong to the person who just got out of that vehicle. Your situational awareness is compromised because you failed to recognise the change in your environment: the transition from a passive observer to a potential threat.

The key to overcoming change blindness is to train yourself to scan your environment actively. Notice small details, periodically check behind you and trust your instincts if something feels off. The more aware you are, the less likely you are to miss subtle but crucial changes that could impact your safety.

Central vision versus peripheral vision

Our vision is divided into two main types: central vision (main vision) and peripheral vision (side vision). Each plays a different role in how we perceive the world, and understanding these differences is crucial for improving our situational awareness and response time in everyday life.

Here are the differences between the two:

1. Central vision: The focused detail viewer

Our central vision is the sharpest and most detailed part of our eyesight, which allows us to recognise faces, read text and focus on specific objects with clarity. It covers an angle of roughly 30 degrees in front of us, and it acts as our high-definition (HD) vision due to the dense concentration of photoreceptor cells in the fovea, which is a small but powerful part of the retina.[20]

This area of vision relies primarily on cones, which are specialist light-sensitive cells that function best in bright conditions and let us perceive colour and fine details. Our brains process these focused images rapidly, which enables us to react to subtle but crucial details in our environment. Without our central vision, everyday tasks such as reading, identifying faces and tracking moving objects would become extremely difficult. It's this sharp, precise vision that allows us to navigate the world with confidence and awareness.[21,22]

2. Peripheral vision: The wide-angle detector

Our peripheral vision extends beyond our central focus, and it acts as an early warning system for detecting movement and maintaining spatial awareness.[23] By covering a wide field of view – approximately 120–140 degrees – it allows us to sense motion, shapes and changes in our surroundings, without the need to look directly at them.[24]

Unlike our central vision, which provides sharp detail, our peripheral vision is blurry and less defined due to the lower concentration of photoreceptors in the outer retina. Instead of relying on cones for colour and fine details, it's dominated by rods, which are far more sensitive to low light. This gives our peripheral vision a distinct advantage with respect to night vision and motion detection, and it helps us to process movement faster than with central vision.[25,26,27]

This ability makes our peripheral vision critical for situational awareness; it helps us notice potential threats, approaching objects and sudden changes in our environment before we consciously focus on them. Whether it's sensing someone walking behind us, spotting a car approaching from the side or detecting a subtle shift in a crowded space, our peripheral vision is a silent but powerful ally in staying aware and alert.

This means our vision is key – but knowing how to use it effectively is equally important. As a former police officer, I was trained as an advanced driver, which meant I learned how to scan my surroundings, identify hazards and anticipate potential dangers before they became a threat. This same approach applies when we're walking out and about in everyday life.

Instead of walking around with tunnel vision, train yourself to take in as much information as possible. Look up and scan your environment, especially in low-light conditions. Check to your sides, and glance into mirrors and reflective surfaces (such as shop windows) to see what's behind you.

Keep your awareness broad – knowing what's there and who's there is half the battle.

The more you practice active observation, the more natural it becomes. Over time, your subconscious will start working with you, alerting you to potential dangers before you consciously register them. And that – your gut instinct backed up by awareness – is one of the most powerful tools you have.

Hearing

Hearing is a powerful but often overlooked tool for situational awareness. Unlike our vision, which is limited to what's in our line of sight, sound surrounds us; this provides a constant stream of information about our environment – even when we're not looking.

Training ourselves to listen actively and focus on key sounds can significantly improve our awareness. Our brains naturally filter out background noise, but we can train them to tune in to specific sounds.[28,29] That way, we can detect potential dangers, approaching footsteps, sudden silence or changes in tone – all of which can signal something is off. The more we practice sharpening this sense, the more instinctively we'll react to the world around us, even before we consciously recognise a threat.

How our brains process sound

Sound is a constant flow of information, but our brains don't process all of it equally. Instead, they act as natural filters that prioritise what's important while tuning out background noise. Without this ability, we'd be overwhelmed by the sheer volume of auditory input around us. This selective processing is a crucial survival mechanism, which allows us to react quickly to danger, recognise familiar voices and navigate our surroundings without conscious effort.[30,31]

Unlike vision, which requires us to look in a specific direction, sound provides 360-degree awareness that alerts us to things happening behind us or beyond our line of sight. We react to sudden loud noises faster than visual stimuli,[32] which is an instinct rooted in survival. Our hearing is also finely tuned to mid-range frequencies[33] – such as human voices, alarms and footsteps – which ensures these critical sounds stand out, even in noisy environments. Incredibly, the human brain can distinguish hundreds of thousands of variations in sound[34] – recognising subtle differences in tone, pitch and intensity.

By understanding how our brains process sound, we can train ourselves to listen more effectively. Paying closer attention to specific noises – such as changes in footsteps, a sudden silence or an unusual sound in the distance – can enhance our situational awareness and help us react more rapidly to potential threats before we even see them.

Understanding white noise and sound filtering

White noise is a steady, unstructured sound that contains all frequencies at equal intensity, much like white light contains all visible wavelengths. It blends individual sounds into a continuous hum, which creates an auditory backdrop that our brains naturally tune out. Everyday examples include the whir of an air conditioner, ocean waves, distant traffic or even TV static – all of which are sounds that fade into the background over time.

This process, called 'auditory habituation', is where our brains filter out repetitive, non-threatening noises to prevent sensory overload; it's why we stop noticing the ticking of a clock, why city residents can sleep through honking horns while a visitor finds them disruptive, and why workers in loud factory environments adjust to the constant machinery noises.[35,36] While this filtering mechanism helps us focus on more-relevant sounds, it can also make us unaware of subtle audio cues – which is an issue when we're trying to stay situationally aware.

Why dangerous sounds stand out

Our brains are hardwired to detect sounds that signal potential danger, which is a survival mechanism that's deeply rooted in our fight-or-flight response. Unlike ordinary background noises, certain auditory cues demand immediate attention, which triggers an instinctive reaction before we even have time to think.[37,38]

2 – SITUATIONAL AWARENESS : THE POWER OF PERCEPTION

Sudden, sharp noises – such as a bang or a scream – instantly break through distractions, forcing us to focus. High-pitched, piercing sounds – such as a siren, an alarm or a baby's cry – cut through the ambient noise, making them impossible to ignore. Repetitive patterns – such as a continuous car horn or a smoke alarm – create a sense of urgency that signals something is wrong. Our brains are also remarkably skilled at pinpointing the direction of danger, which helps us react quickly to a potential threat.[39,40,41]

This instinctive response plays out in everyday life. A parent will wake instantly to the sound of their baby crying, even while they're sleeping through a thunderstorm. A driver, despite the hum of the road and the music in the background, will immediately register the sound of a honking horn. In a combat situation – which is a high-stakes environment – soldiers are trained to distinguish between routine noise and sounds that signal an immediate threat, such as gunfire or approaching footsteps.

Turn your hearing into a superpower

Most people don't realise they can enhance their hearing simply by altering how they collect sound. The larger the surface area of the ear, the more sound waves it captures, which makes it easier to interpret distant noises, conversations and subtle sounds we might otherwise miss.

We know dogs have superior auditory sensitivity compared to humans, particularly at higher frequencies; they can detect quieter sounds and hear ultrasonic frequencies up to 60,000 Hz – which is three times higher than the human upper limit of 20,000 Hz – and this enables them to perceive faint or distant noises that humans would likely miss.[42] And cats have even more advanced hearing, which is tuned to higher frequencies that help them detect prey.[43] But what if you could amplify your own hearing? It's easier than you think. By simply cupping your hands around your ears and pushing them forward, you mimic the effect of having standing, forward-facing ears – like a dog or a cat. Try it. You'll instantly notice that sounds become clearer and more defined. Even the muffled voices of distant people can transform into recognisable words.

To fine-tune your directional hearing, turn your head or adjust your cupped ears toward the sound. If you're near a wall, tree or rock face, you can amplify the sound further by cupping your hand around your ear and angling it toward the solid surface, as the sound waves will bounce off the surface and be channelled into your ear.

I use this technique all the time, and it gives me an edge in awareness. Whether I'm listening for footsteps behind me or picking up on conversations in the distance, this simple trick allows me to detect things much sooner than if I relied on my regular hearing alone.

Practice active listening and stay aware

When walking alone, ditch the distractions. Take your earphones out of your ears, or if you must use them, choose ones that still let you hear your surroundings. Your awareness starts with sound – and the way you process it could be the difference between staying safe and being caught off guard.

Listen to any footsteps behind you. Are they soft or heavy? Do they sound like wide strides (which would suggest a taller person, possibly a man)? Pay attention to whether they're matching your pace – this is a huge red flag. Humans naturally walk with their

2 – SITUATIONAL AWARENESS : THE POWER OF PERCEPTION

own rhythm; we never perfectly sync our steps with someone else unless we're deliberately trying to. If someone is mirroring your stride, cross the road. If they follow, slow down. If they slow too, they're almost certainly following you. No one does this by accident.

One simple trick is to stop abruptly and pretend to check your phone as if you've forgotten something. A normal passerby will continue walking, but if this person lingers or stops too, they're watching you. Another tactic is to make direct eye contact with them – this is one of the most effective ways to put someone off. It forces them to acknowledge that you've seen them, which strips them of the element of surprise. Most offenders thrive on catching their victims unaware; eye contact alone can make them reconsider their intentions.

But what if they still don't leave? If they hesitate nearby, pretend to use their phone or fidget with their shoelaces, trust your instincts – you're being followed. If it's safe, take a photo discreetly and call the police immediately. Give them your exact location and a clear description of the person, speaking loudly enough that your follower will hear you. This shows them you're aware and taking action.

Your best defence is movement and space – never let yourself become boxed in. If you feel unsafe, head to a public area, a shop, a mall or a row of houses. Look for places with lights on, CCTV cameras or Ring doorbells (or similar). Avoid going straight home, as you don't want them to learn where you live. Prioritise visibility, control and distance, because awareness is your first line of defence.

Smell

Smell is a powerful but often overlooked tool for detecting who or what is around us. We may not always realise it, but our sense of smell can provide an early warning system for potential dangers – especially in situations where our vision is limited, such as in low light or complete darkness.

Exactly as my dad taught me when I was younger, I make a habit of noticing scents and linking them to specific people or places. While sight and hearing are our dominant senses for awareness, smell can alert us to someone's presence long before we actually see them. Start by practising: pay attention to the smells around you as you walk through your neighbourhood, a park or a city street. Identify familiar scents such as perfume, aftershave, cigarette smoke or vape vapour, and try to match them with the people nearby. You might notice that you can identify five different scents but see only four people – which means someone else is nearby but out of sight.

If you smell cigarette smoke but can't see the smoker, this could indicate someone is hiding close by. In these moments, pay attention to the wind direction; observe trees, bushes or other movement in the environment to determine where the scent is coming from. Smells often travel in the same direction as the breeze, unless the wind is too strong or erratic – in which case, it may disperse unpredictably.

Beyond detecting people, smell can also alert you to other dangers, such as fire, gas leaks or even distressed animals. Train yourself to notice and process smells instinctively – the more you practice, the more second nature it becomes.

Taste

Our sense of taste is an evolutionary safeguard; that is, a built-in defence mechanism designed to detect toxins before they can harm us. Bitterness, in particular, is often associated with danger, as many poisonous plants and substances contain natural toxins that have an unpleasant taste. Throughout history, humans have relied on this instinct to avoid dangerous foods, and while we may not be foraging for survival today, our ability to recognise off-tasting substances is still just as crucial.[44,45]

Beyond nature, many chemical compounds, heavy metals and industrial agents also have distinct bitter or metallic flavours when ingested.[46,47] Even certain drugs and poisons have been intentionally formulated to taste unpleasant as a deterrent. But in modern society, this instinct is even more vital for protecting ourselves from intentional tampering – especially when it comes to food and drink safety.

Taste can serve as an early warning sign if something isn't right. If a drink suddenly tastes unusually bitter, metallic or off, it could indicate it's been spiked or contaminated. Likewise, a sudden change in the taste of water – whether chlorine-like, overly sweet or chemical – may signal pollution or even an attempt to drug it. The same applies to food; a strange texture or unexpected taste could indicate spoilage or, in rare cases, intentional interference. If something tastes wrong, trust your instincts – don't consume it. Return a questionable drink, order a fresh one or simply walk away.

I once experienced this firsthand. Someone I felt uneasy around insisted on buying me a drink. Not wanting to be rude, I took a sip, but instead of swallowing, I let the liquid sit on my tongue for a moment. Something wasn't right. Instead of reacting outright, I casually said, "Oh, I think this is diet cola; I asked for regular." This gave me a perfect excuse to return it to the waitress and get a new one. The replacement drink tasted normal, but more importantly, I noticed a shift in the person's body language: they suddenly became tense and uneasy. That was all the confirmation I needed. They'd tampered with my drink, and I was getting the hell out of there.

> *Your taste and instincts work together -- so trust them. If something seems off, don't ignore it. Your safety is always more important than politeness.*

CHAPTER 3

Body Language

Body language is a fascinating but complex subject; you could study it for years and still second-guess what you see. People are unique, and while physical cues can reveal a lot, interpreting them accurately requires context. A stranger acting oddly may be anxious, neurodivergent or genuinely have bad intentions. Facial expressions, eye movements and gestures are often used to detect deception, but reading people effectively will depend on recognising deviations from their usual behaviour.

For example, just because someone's eye twitches while speaking doesn't mean they're lying; it could be a nervous tic or a stress reaction. The key is establishing a baseline – that is, the way someone normally acts – so when they behave differently, it stands out. The better you know a person, the easier it is to detect these changes.

Detecting deception through body language

When people lie, their bodies often betray them. While skilled deceivers may suppress obvious cues, subconscious behaviours can still give them away. Some common signs of dishonesty include avoiding eye contact, excessive blinking or giving unnecessary details to sound more convincing. Pausing too long before answering may indicate they're buying time to fabricate a lie, while fidgeting or touching their face can be signs of nervousness.[48,49]

I once noticed a colleague yawning every time I asked about his weekend. At first, I thought nothing of it, but I realised he only did this when answering certain questions. To test my theory, I switched between casual topics and asking about his weekend; each time I brought his weekend up, he yawned again. Later, I discovered he'd been keeping it secret that he was having an affair!

Sometimes, the smallest physical cues can reveal the most.

Spotting bad intentions and aggression

I learned a lot about this in my training as a police officer. Body language can also warn you if someone is preparing for aggressive action, hiding a weapon or planning something sinister. Hands are particularly revealing. A person reaching for a concealed object may repeatedly touch a certain spot on their body, much like how people instinctively check their pocket for a passport when travelling. Feet can also give away intent – if someone's feet are angled toward an exit while engaging in a conversation, they may be planning a quick getaway.[50,51]

Pre-violence indicators are often subtle but crucial. Clenching fists, flared nostrils, deep breathing and a sudden, unnatural stillness can each signal an impending attack. Lowering the head while staring up is a classic predatory look, and removing items such as a jacket or watch may indicate someone preparing for a physical altercation.[52,53,54]

3 – BODY LANGUAGE

The importance of context

Interpreting body language isn't about jumping to conclusions; it's about recognising patterns and trusting your instincts. Again, I learned a lot about this in my work as a police officer. A twitchy stranger could be lying, or they could simply be nervous. Someone adjusting their waistband might simply be fixing their clothes – or checking for a weapon. Context is everything. The more you practice observation, the more attuned you become to reading people accurately and staying one step ahead. You'll find this easier to do with people you know. So even if you think you know someone, if they're giving off some of these cues, then it's time to act. Make space and stay away from them.

What about our own body language?

Studies have shown that criminals don't select their victims randomly; instead, they subconsciously assess body language and nonverbal cues to determine who appears weak, distracted or unaware. One well-known study by researchers Betty Grayson and Morris I. Stein explored this concept by showing a group of convicted criminals footage of people walking down the street.[55] The criminals were asked to identify who they would target for robbery or assault, and remarkably, they all selected the same individuals. Surprisingly, their choices weren't based purely on physical size, gender or age – instead, they focused on how people moved and how they carried themselves.

The study found that people who walked hesitantly, with shuffling steps or poor posture, were chosen more frequently. Those who avoided eye contact, looked down at their phones or seemed unaware of their surroundings were also easy targets.[56] Criminals instinctively seek out individuals who appear weak or distracted, because they seem less likely to put up a fight or recognise a threat in sufficient time to react. On the other hand, individuals who walked with confidence, kept their heads up and displayed strong posture were rarely selected.

This research highlights an important reality: your body language can either deter or invite danger. Walking with purpose, keeping your shoulders back and staying alert can signal to potential predators that you aren't an easy victim. Something as simple as making brief eye contact with those around you, instead of looking down at your phone, can make all the difference. Criminals want an easy target, and by projecting confidence and awareness, you can drastically reduce your chances of being singled out by them.

Your gut instinct: The sixth sense

As a former police officer, I'm familiar with something often called a 'policeman's nose' or gut feeling. It's an instinct – a deep, unexplainable knowing – that led me to people who were hiding, warned me when something bad was about to happen or gave me that unmistakeable sense something was off. It's like a prewarning system or an awareness of danger before we consciously understand why.

Our sixth sense is this instinctual awareness – an ability to process subtle cues, patterns and changes without consciously thinking about them. It plays a huge role in safety, decision-making and reading people's intentions, even when we can't quite explain why we feel a certain way.

So how does the sixth sense actually work? Our brains are constantly scanning for signals – body language, facial expressions, tone of voice and environmental shifts – and processing this information at a subconscious level. While much of our situational awareness relies on active observation, our gut instinct works in the background, catching things before we fully register them.[57,58,59]

Have you ever met someone and immediately felt uneasy, despite them being polite? Walked into a room and sensed tension before anyone spoke? Known someone was lying, even though you had no logical reason to think so? These feelings aren't random; they come from micro-expressions, inconsistencies and subtle details that your subconscious picks up faster than your conscious mind can process.

So far, we've explored practical intuition, but what about the other side of the sixth sense? Do we possess something beyond what science can explain?

This isn't a book about spirituality, but it would be naïve to dismiss the experiences of so many people who feel guided by intuition, guardian angels or ancestral protectors. If you believe in spiritual guidance, why not use that belief to your advantage?

One thing I've heard repeatedly is that we have free will, and because of this, the spirit world requires our permission to step in. If this idea resonates with you, then ask for protection, guidance and heightened awareness in moments where you feel vulnerable.

Whether you see it as a spiritual safeguard or simply an extra layer of mental reassurance, why not welcome every possible advantage? If there's even a chance that something unseen is watching out for you, it's worth calling upon.

Keeping-safe tips

If you're on foot and suspect someone is following you, change your pace.

CHAPTER 4

Am I Being Followed?

If you think you're being followed, trust your instincts – you're probably right. With heightened situational awareness, you'll already be noticing more than ever before, and now it's time to put that awareness into action.

If you're on foot and suspect someone is following you, change your pace. A normal pedestrian will either overtake you or slow down more than you – people naturally dislike walking at the exact same speed as the person in front of them. If the person behind you matches your pace, that's a red flag. The same principle applies to vehicles – drivers don't typically stay side by side or at the exact same distance behind you. If you suspect you're being tailed while driving, change direction. On a major road or motorway, exit at the next junction and rejoin. If they do the same, you have confirmation. If you're on a country road, don't drive home; instead, head to a busy public area or a police station. This will usually deter them.

In the UK, you can't legally use a mobile phone while driving, except to call the emergency services. If you believe you're being followed, call 999 immediately, but don't stop moving.

On foot, one of the simplest tactics is to cross the road, pretend to forget something (for example, check where your phone is), or even turn around completely and go in the opposite direction, then casually observe their reaction. If they hesitate or awkwardly amend their route, they're making a split-second decision about what to do next. Use this moment to look them in the eye; a direct stare can be enough to put them off. Memorise their clothing, build and key features, and check if anyone else nearby seems connected to them. But don't stop for long – keep moving.

If you suspect you're being followed, pay close attention to their footwear. Jackets, hats and sunglasses can easily be changed to alter someone's appearance, but shoes are rarely switched. Also, study their gait – everyone has a unique way of walking. In the same way as you can recognise a friend from a distance by their stride, you can use this skill to identify someone who may be following you, even if they change outfits.

The reality of stalking in the UK

In England and Wales, one in seven people aged 16 and above reported having experienced stalking in 2024; that's 1.5 million victims.[60] To help us understand the scale of stalking in the UK, if we divide that 1.5 million victims by the 365 days in a year, we get an average of around 4,110 people experiencing stalking each day. Going back to our earlier London double-decker bus example – where the New Routemaster model can hold around 87 passengers[61] – we can see that *47 double-decker buses' worth* of people experience stalking *every single day*. To put this into further perspective: there are 1,440 minutes in a day, and if we divide those 1,440 minutes by 47 buses, we get roughly *one full bus of victims every 30 minutes* – all day, every day, throughout the year. The numbers alone highlight that stalking is a very real and present threat.

Stalking is often misunderstood as someone simply being followed, but in reality, it encompasses a wide range of unwanted, persistent and distressing behaviours. According to the Crown Prosecution Service (CPS) and the Protection from Harassment Act 1997,[62] stalking includes not only physical following but also repeated and intrusive actions such as unwanted communication (e.g. texts, emails or phone calls), spying, loitering, property damage, threats, and even cyberstalking through social media or GPS tracking. These behaviours are often designed to instil fear, exert control or maintain unwanted contact – and they can escalate over time if left unchallenged.

In fact, research shows that the psychological impact of stalking is often more damaging than any physical confrontation, with victims frequently reporting anxiety, depression, PTSD symptoms, and significant disruptions to their daily life and work.[63] Many victims don't immediately identify what they're experiencing as stalking – particularly when the behaviour involves someone they know – until the cumulative impact becomes overwhelming. Acknowledging this broader definition is essential to understanding the true scale and seriousness of stalking in the UK. And understanding the full scope of stalking is essential if we're to take it seriously, protect ourselves and support others effectively.

As we move through the next chapters, we'll shift from raising awareness to building preparedness. You'll learn practical tools to strengthen your situational awareness, help you recognise early warning signs, and enable you to respond confidently if you or someone you know encounters stalking or similar controlling behaviours.

> *Empowerment begins not only with knowledge but also with taking the right steps early and safely.*

CHAPTER 5

The Unwritten Contract

Over the years, I've learned that some of the most dangerous traps aren't the ones shouted from the rooftops; it's the ones whispered in the form of kindness. They come disguised as generosity. As gifts. But behind the pretty wrapping, there's often an invisible price tag – an unwritten contract.

Years ago, I was on holiday in Kenya, soaking in the beauty of the landscape and the warmth of the people. During an amazing safari, our guide took us to witness a traditional Maasai warrior dance. It was mesmerising, with the colours, the rhythm and the proud movements of the dancers.

At the end of the performance, each tourist was handed a beaded necklace, which was presented as a gift. At first, I declined politely, but I was told it would be deeply disrespectful to refuse something that had been blessed. So I smiled and accepted it, feeling touched by the gesture.

However, just moments later, a request followed for a 'gift' in return – specifically in the form of US dollars or British pounds. My gut had already sensed it. What looked like generosity was actually a transaction – an exchange – and I'd unknowingly signed the contract by accepting.

That experience has stayed with me. Not because of the money, but because it was the first time I truly understood how people can use generosity as a trap. Over the years, I've seen this play out in countless ways – especially as a woman. Last year, I had a moment that brought it all back.

I was at a bar with a friend, catching up, laughing and simply enjoying a night out. While waiting to order our drinks, a man standing nearby offered to buy one for me.

I smiled and said, "No thanks, I've already ordered."

He persisted: "It's okay; I'll get it."

"It's fine; I'm buying for my friend too," I replied, trying to keep it light.

Then his tone changed. "Bloody hell, just take the drink," he snapped.

I turned to him and calmly but firmly said, "It's never just a drink. It's a contract. If I take your drink, I'm expected to smile and say thank you. Then you'll want to talk. And then it turns into you thinking I owe you my time, my attention and maybe even more. I don't want to talk to you. I'm here with a friend. I'm not interested."

His face twisted in anger. That reaction told me everything I needed to know. He then insulted me, which is a classic deflection. And when I pointed out the wedding ring on his finger and said I felt sorry for his wife, he blew up even more.

Now I know I poked the bear with that last comment, but I'd had enough. I've learned that standing your ground doesn't always come without backlash, but it's always worth it.

5 – THE UNWRITTEN CONTRACT

So here's my advice, especially to younger women or anyone still learning to listen to that inner voice. If someone you don't know offers you a drink, don't accept it. Not at a bar, not at a party and not from a stranger's hand. Because it's rarely a gift. It's a lead-in. A hook. A set-up for something you didn't ask for.

Even worse, if someone sends you a drink you didn't watch being made, walk away. You don't know what's in it.

You don't owe anyone politeness at the cost of your safety.

That free drink? It might cost you a lot more than £10.

Keeping-safe tips

Learning self-defence can be empowering.

CHAPTER 6

Environmental Conditions

From what I've witnessed, bad weather causes more burglaries, but it's not just due to the wind and rain itself – it's what comes with it. In the winter months, burglary rates in the UK can rise by up to 40%,[64] and that's mostly down to the longer, darker nights. When it's cold, wet and miserable outside, fewer people are walking around, which gives burglars more freedom to move without being seen. Add to that the howling wind and heavy rain, and it's easy to mistake the sound of a window breaking for just another bin being blown over. Suspicious noises are brushed off, and people are more likely to stay indoors and mind their own business. It all creates the perfect cover for someone who doesn't want to be noticed. This is why securing your home is even more critical in poor weather. Lock your doors and windows, and also eliminate potential hiding spots – those large, beautiful bushes around the side of your house may look great, but they also provide cover for someone lying in wait. Installing motion-activated lights in these areas can act as a deterrent and improve your safety when returning home.

While bad weather brings more burglaries, good weather fuels violent crime. The long summer days and rising temperatures increase alcohol and drug use, which leads to more aggression and a spike in violent offences. And while we often focus on the risks posed by others, we also need to consider our own alcohol consumption.

I love a night out as much as the next girl, but I always make sure I'm sensible when walking home through the city. We must look out for each other too – because we all know that one friend who drinks too much and becomes a liability. It's tempting to leave them to deal with their own mess, but don't. Talk about it in the morning, but while you're out, stick together and make sure everyone gets home safe.

When it comes to getting home safely, I never take unnecessary risks. If I'm in the city, I've had a few drinks and I want fresh air, I'll walk home the long way, sticking to well-lit streets with bars, shops and CCTV. But if I'm in a rural area or unsure of the safest route, I take a real taxi. And I never accept lifts from strangers, no matter how friendly or helpful they seem.

Another growing concern is spiking. Between 2022 and 2023, the UK recorded 6,732 reports of drink and needle spiking,[65] yet it's estimated that up to 90% of cases go unreported.[66] This means the true scale of the problem is far larger than official statistics suggest. Once spiked, whether you're male or female, there's no stopping the effects. If you suspect a friend is acting strangely, confused or suddenly out of control, stop drinking immediately and get help.

6 – ENVIRONMENTAL CONDITIONS

Not all dangers come from outside

Unfortunately, not all threats come from strangers. Many dangers exist within the home and among people we trust. In the UK, one in four women will experience some form of sexual violence in their lifetime.[67] In the past year alone, 1.6 million women have reported domestic abuse,[68] and 80 women were allegedly killed by men[69] – which is an average of one woman every three days.[70] Alarmingly, 61% of victims were killed by a current or former partner, and 90% of perpetrators were someone the victim knew.[71]

So how can we protect ourselves from violence at home or by someone we trust?

The first step is to recognise the early warning signs. Flashes in temper or controlling behaviour – such as excessive jealousy, monitoring of activities, or isolation from friends and family – is often a precursor to abuse. Verbal abuse, frequent criticism and demeaning comments can escalate into physical violence. Trust your instincts; *if something feels wrong, it probably is.*

Having a safety plan can be lifesaving. Identify safe spaces where you can go in an emergency, such as a friend's house or a public place. Keep emergency contacts saved in your phone, and establish a code word with trusted people to signal when you need immediate help. Technology can also be a powerful tool; safety apps can alert your contacts and record evidence, while wearable devices can automatically notify the emergency services if distress is detected.

For legal protection, restraining orders (protective orders) can prevent an abuser from contacting or approaching a victim. These legally enforceable measures provide an added layer of security.

Women escaping abuse can also seek help from shelters and support organisations such as Refuge, which provides emergency accommodation, counselling and advocacy. The main problem is that these only usually take effect once something has happened. If you're noticing something that's off with someone you know, speak up. If you're young, speak up and tell someone, and if you're scared of telling a family member, then speak with a teacher at school or a friend's mum. The more people you tell, the better.

Learning self-defence can be empowering. Women's self-defence training helps build confidence and provides practical techniques to help you escape dangerous situations. Around the world, programmes such as those in Kenya's Maasai communities are teaching girls to defend themselves against sexual abuse and forced marriage – which is a reminder that knowledge and training can make a difference.

Having a strong support network is vital. Confiding in your friends, family or professionals can provide you with emotional and practical help. Counselling services offer coping strategies and support in rebuilding self-esteem. Education is key, so learning about the dynamics of abuse and the available resources can prepare you to recognise and respond to danger. Community workshops and safety programmes can also provide valuable tools for empowerment and protection.

CHAPTER 7

Fight or Flight

Have you ever felt your heart race when you're scared? Or had the sudden urge to run away from a stressful situation? Maybe you've even found yourself frozen in place, unable to react. These automatic responses – fight, flight, freeze and flop – are the body's way of handling perceived danger, all controlled by the sympathetic nervous system (SNS).[72,73]

We've all heard of 'fight or flight', but human responses to fear go beyond those two. The brain sometimes decides that fighting or running isn't an option, which can lead to freezing – or even a complete shutdown, which is known as the 'flop' response. These reactions are deeply wired into our biology, and they shape how we respond to danger and influence our ability to assess situations clearly.

How our bodies react to stress

When the brain senses danger, it doesn't stop to ask whether the threat is real or imagined – it reacts. The amygdala, which is the part of the brain that processes emotions, kicks into high gear and sends distress signals to the body.

When this happens to you, a wave of physiological changes sweeps over you almost instantly:

- Your heart rate spikes, which pumps more blood to your muscles.
- Your breathing quickens, which fuels your body with extra oxygen.
- Your pupils dilate, which sharpens your vision.
- Stress hormones such as adrenaline and cortisol flood your system, putting you on high alert.

These changes are designed to help us react quickly, but while they can boost our ability to respond to danger, they can also cloud our judgement, which makes it harder to think clearly or assess the full picture.

The four stress responses

The fight response: When we stand our ground

Sometimes, our bodies decide that the best way to handle a threat is to confront it head-on. This is the *fight* response, where we feel a surge of energy and aggression as we get ready to take action. Our bodies prepare us to defend ourselves, whether that means fighting physically, arguing or pushing back against a challenge.

While the fight response sharpens our focus on the threat, it can create tunnel vision, which blocks out important details about the situation. This can make us miss escape routes, misjudge the level of danger or act impulsively.

The flight response: When escape is the best option

When we're faced with danger, running away is sometimes the smartest choice. The *flight* response prepares our bodies to escape:

our muscles tense, adrenaline surges and our mind scans for a way out.

This response can heighten our alertness, which helps us notice exits or escape routes. But panic can also take over, which leads to us making hasty, irrational decisions – such as running without a clear plan or overlooking other dangers in the environment.

The freeze response: When we can't move

Have you ever felt completely stuck in fear, as though your body simply won't respond? That's the *freeze* response. Instead of fighting or fleeing, the brain signals the body to shut down movement. This can be someone going silent, feeling paralysed or being unable to think clearly. It's our bodies' way of avoiding detection – playing 'invisible' in the hope that the danger will pass.

Freezing can make us lose track of what's happening, which causes delayed reactions or difficulty making decisions. It can also instigate us missing clear escape opportunities.

The flop response: When our bodies completely shut down

A step beyond freezing is the *flop* response, where our bodies go limp – sometimes even collapsing. This survival instinct is often seen in instances of extreme fear or trauma. It can happen when we feel completely overwhelmed, powerless or in shock.

Flopping leaves us completely vulnerable, with an unresponsive body and a foggy mind. In dangerous situations, this can make it impossible to react or escape.

Regaining control

Understanding these responses can help us recognise when they're happening and learn ways to regain control. Simple techniques –

for instance, grounding exercises, controlled breathing or shifting our focus to external details – can help us override these instinctive reactions, which gives us back the power to respond effectively.

> *The next time you feel your body reacting to stress, try to pause and notice whether you're fighting, fleeing, freezing or flopping. Recognising these responses is the first step to managing them – so you can take control, rather than letting them take control of you.*

The least effective responses in a dangerous situation are freeze and flop, because they leave you vulnerable and unable to escape. If you know you tend to react in this way, focus on movement – even small actions can help break the paralysis. The more you move, the harder you are to target. Keep going, stay aware and get yourself to safety as quickly as possible.

CHAPTER 8

Training for Survival:
The Power of Movement, Self-Defence and Muscle Memory

In high-stress situations, movement equals survival. Whether we're facing an attacker, a sudden emergency or an overwhelming moment of fear, if we keep moving, we have a significantly higher chance of making it out safely.[74,75,76] However, when adrenaline surges and panic sets in, our brains can slow down, which makes it difficult to think clearly or react effectively. This is where martial arts, self-defence training and muscle memory become crucial. When our bodies have been trained to respond through repetition, movement becomes automatic, which eliminates hesitation and ensures the right actions happen instinctively – even under extreme pressure.

Muscle memory is the key to reacting without thinking. When we've practised a movement – whether it's breaking free from a grab, blocking a strike or executing an escape manoeuvre – enough times, it becomes deeply embedded in our nervous systems. Instead of needing to decide consciously how to respond, our bodies simply act. This is critical because hesitation can be fatal in life-threatening situations. As discussed, the freeze or flop response can cause our brains to stall, leaving us vulnerable. However, if we're trained, we can override this response by acting instinctively – our training takes over before fear can paralyse us.

Staying in motion also makes us a harder target. Criminals prefer victims who are distracted, hesitant or frozen in fear. Someone who moves confidently, reacts quickly and refuses to be stationary is far more difficult to control or harm. Martial arts training reinforces this principle by teaching students how to angle their bodies, evade grabs and maintain awareness of their surroundings. Techniques such as quick footwork, evasive manoeuvres and controlled movement allow trained individuals to avoid being cornered or overpowered.

Situational awareness and self-defence go hand in hand. A trained individual doesn't just react better; they see danger before it happens. Through martial arts, we can learn to read body language, recognise potential threats and respond without hesitation. The movements become second nature, which allows us to stay one step ahead of danger. Instead of being caught off guard, we could instinctively position ourselves for escape or defence, making us far less vulnerable in a confrontation.

In moments of danger, there's no time to think; there's only time to act. Your body will only do what it has been trained to do. Self-defence, martial arts and movement training ensure that, when fear and adrenaline take over, your response is immediate, automatic and effective. The more you've practised reacting to threats, the less likely you are to freeze or hesitate. Muscle memory turns training into a survival instinct, which ensures movement isn't just a choice but is a reflex.

For me, self-defence classes or martial arts are an absolute must. As soon as my siblings and I were old enough, our dad sent us to karate lessons, and it was one of the best things he ever did for us. Beyond learning how to fight, it instilled confidence, self-awareness, discipline and resilience in us. It's also an incredible form of exercise that strengthens both the body and mind.

Even as a police officer, I've found myself effectively restraining and arresting suspects using techniques I first learned as a teenager. Martial arts aren't only about fighting – they're about control, strategy and using an opponent's force against them. That's why law enforcement agencies across the world incorporate martial arts into their training. With the right techniques, even the smallest person can overpower a much larger attacker, all while staying as safe as possible.

Another crucial lesson martial arts teaches us is knowing your limits. Overconfidence can be dangerous: I've seen countless people who thought they were tough only to find themselves in situations their arrogance couldn't get them out of. True strength lies in caution, awareness and the ability to assess a situation before it escalates. *A trained person doesn't just know how to fight; they know when not to.*

> *One thing I'd encourage everyone to do is to learn self-defence. It's not about looking for a fight; it's about ensuring you can protect yourself and those around you when it matters most.*

Know where you are: The importance of location awareness in emergencies

One of the most critical aspects of personal safety is knowing exactly where you are at all times. In an emergency, whether you need to escape a dangerous situation, call for help or assist someone else, having a strong awareness of your surroundings can mean the difference between life and death. The same as on an aeroplane when passengers are instructed before take-off to note the nearest exits, being aware of emergency exits, street names and entry points in everyday situations is a vital survival skill.

When you step into any new environment – a shopping mall, hotel, restaurant or even a crowded public space – make it a habit to locate the nearest exits. In a crisis, such as a fire, an attack or a sudden panic situation, the natural human instinct is to rush back the way we came. But what if that path is blocked? People who take note of multiple exits ahead of time have a far higher chance of escaping safely. Whether you're indoors or outdoors, always give yourself options. Look for emergency doors, stairwells and secondary exits in case you can't use the main entrance.

The same principle applies when walking through unfamiliar streets. Take mental notes of street names, landmarks and notable intersections as you move. In a dangerous situation, you may need to call for help and tell the authorities exactly where you are. Saying, "I'm near a shop with a blue sign," is far less useful than being able to say, "I'm on Marine Parade, outside the Grand Hotel." If you're in a foreign country where street signs may not be obvious, identify unique landmarks or take quick mental snapshots of your route. This way, if you need to retrace your steps or direct someone to your location, you won't be lost or disoriented.

Emergencies don't always happen in isolated areas. Crowded events, music festivals and public transport stations can become chaotic in moments of crisis. In situations where a large number of people are suddenly trying to escape – such as a fire, an active shooter or a terrorist attack – being aware of alternative exits and safe zones allows you to act quickly and decisively while others hesitate. The people who panic first are often those who don't know where to go. The ones who survive are those who've already mapped out a way to safety before they needed it.

Beyond purely safety reasons, location awareness is also essential for calling for help. If you ever need to dial the emergency services, your ability to describe your location quickly and accurately will determine how fast help arrives. Every second matters in a crisis, and the police, paramedics or fire service can only respond efficiently if they know exactly where you are. The faster they find you, the better your chances of survival.

> *Teaching yourself to be aware of your surroundings isn't about paranoia; it's about being prepared.*

Just as pilots and flight attendants emphasise emergency procedures before take-off on an aeroplane, you should make it a personal habit to stay alert, note exits and mentally track your location everywhere you go. *The key to survival is being ready before disaster strikes, not after.* Train yourself to always know where you are, and you'll never be truly lost.

Keeping-safe tips

A personal safety alarm is a great tool to carry with you.

CHAPTER 9

What to Carry for Protection

In the UK, it's illegal to carry an item specifically for self-defence. This means that, while in other parts of the world, I would recommend something like a tactical pen, UK law prevents carrying any object with the sole intent of using it as a weapon. However, that doesn't mean you can't carry everyday items that double as tools for safety.

A tactical pen is a fully functional writing tool, usually made from aircraft-grade aluminium, which makes it lightweight, durable and incredibly strong. Many are designed with a glass-breaker tip, which could, of course, be useful in an emergency. While carrying one for self-defence would be illegal, there's absolutely nothing stopping you from carrying it as a standard pen – it's a subtle, practical item that could offer a last resort if needed.

Another fantastic legal tool is a personal safety alarm. These devices work by either pressing a button or pulling a cord, which triggers an ear-piercing siren that's designed to disorient an attacker and attract attention. They're easy to carry and completely legal, though they do have the downside of going off at the worst possible times if you accidentally trigger them!

Safety apps have become an incredible modern protection tool. With some apps, you can share your walking route with friends, and if you deviate unexpectedly, they receive an immediate alert. Some apps use artificial intelligence and wearable technology to monitor your heart rate and movement patterns, from which they automatically detect sudden distress or erratic movements. If an attack is detected, they can alert your emergency contacts, record evidence and even let you call the emergency services with a single tap.

What do I use?

I walk my dog every morning and night, and like most dog walkers, I have a go-to coat for doing so. Over time, I realised that this routine – though necessary – makes me vulnerable, as anyone observing me could easily identify this pattern. Although I mix up my routes as much as possible, my dog still needs toilet breaks before and after work, which means my timings are often predictable.

Because my dog tends to wander into dark corners to do his business, I carry a torch: an ultra-bright 2000-lumen light. I only carry it to see into alleyways and pick up after my dog. But should someone try to attack me, I know that a quick flash of 2000 lumens into their eyes would blind them temporarily, giving me precious seconds to escape and call the police.

I actually discovered exactly how effective this could be by accident – I once turned the torch on straight into my own eyes, like a complete idiot.

The result?

Instant disorientation and a lesson well learned!

Sometimes, the best defence isn't a weapon; it's simply having the right tools and the awareness to use them effectively.

Keeping-safe tips

If you know you're in a vulnerable situation, stay switched on and adjust your behaviour accordingly.

CHAPTER 10

Recognising Your Most Vulnerable Moments

Understanding when you're the most vulnerable is key to staying safe. For me, one of those times is when I'm walking my dog, particularly in the early morning or late at night, when most people are either asleep or indoors. In the winter months, darkness falls earlier, which makes these routine walks even riskier. That's why I make conscious choices about where I go. I never walk anywhere that feels off, I avoid walking down alleyways, and I always stick to well-lit residential streets.

Another time I'm particularly vulnerable is when I'm walking home after I've been drinking (even after just one or two). Alcohol slows your reaction time and clouds your judgement, which makes it easier to miss warning signs or become a target for opportunistic criminals. Travelling abroad or even being in an unfamiliar area in the UK also increases your vulnerability. When I don't know the layout of a place, it's harder to anticipate safe routes or recognise when something is out of place.

The key is self-awareness. If you know you're in a vulnerable situation, stay switched on and adjust your behaviour accordingly.

Choose safer routes, travel with others when possible and always have a plan for getting home safely. Your instincts and awareness are your first lines of defence – so trust them.

Staying aware before you travel: Avoiding unnecessary risks

Travelling is an exciting experience, but staying safe while you do requires awareness and preparation. Before you set off, take time to understand your destination, know the key locations, learn about local laws and recognise cultural differences, particularly those that may impact your safety.

It's easy to relax too much on holiday, but having a laid-back mindset can dull your situational awareness. You might be familiar with navigating a European city, but what about a country with entirely different laws, customs or social expectations? For women especially, what's acceptable or legal at home may not be the same abroad. A little research can prevent misunderstandings or dangerous situations.

> *One of the simplest ways to stay safe is to blend in rather than stand out.*

Wearing flashy, expensive jewellery and clothes might seem like a harmless way to enjoy a holiday in style, but it also marks you as a prime target for criminals. In unfamiliar environments, thieves, pickpockets and scammers specifically seek out tourists who are displaying wealth. What might feel like an innocent fashion choice can attract unwanted attention, which increases the risk of theft, scams or even violent robbery.

In many popular destinations, pickpockets work in groups, using distraction techniques to steal valuables in seconds. Some criminals even rip necklaces or watches off tourists, often from motorbikes or bicycles, which leaves victims with not only financial loss but also potential injury. Unlike a phone or wallet, jewellery is worn on the body, which makes it harder to let go of if someone tries to snatch it; this can escalate a theft into a violent confrontation.

Beyond crime, wearing expensive jewellery can lead to overcharging and scams. If you obviously look like a wealthy traveller, you may be a target for inflated prices – everywhere from taxis to market vendors. Con artists often take advantage of tourists who appear affluent, leading them into high-pressure sales traps or unsafe situations.

How to travel smart: Practical tips

- **To minimise the risks, dress modestly and avoid flashy displays of wealth:** I keep my accessories simple and practical, and I can enjoy my trips more when I'm not constantly worried about being targeted.
- **Plan your routes before stepping out of your accommodation:** Study a map at your hotel so you have a general awareness of where you're going, rather than stopping in the street to check your phone, which can make you look lost and vulnerable.
- **When using taxis, book one through your hotel rather than hailing one off the street:** Although hotel-arranged taxis may cost more, they're far safer. A hotel has a reputation to protect and will work with reliable services. On the other hand, an unregistered driver from the street may overcharge you, take an unsafe route or worse.
- **Trust the expertise of your hotel staff;** they know their city's risks better than you do.

Keeping-safe tips

If something feels wrong, report it. You never know what piece of information could stop an offender before they escalate.

CHAPTER 11

Report It! Report It! Report It!

This is the part where I get frustrated. Too many crimes go unreported, and it drives me mad. When I was a police officer, I lost count of the number of times people – friends, family and even victims themselves – told me they'd been followed, assaulted or attacked, but they chose not to report it. The reasons varied: they thought it was too minor, they were drunk, they didn't think the police would care or they assumed nothing would be done.

Here's the truth: on its own, your report might not be enough for an arrest, but when combined with other reports, it could be the missing piece that prevents another attack or catches a predator. If someone else was attacked nearby, your information could add weight to their case or help identify patterns. Offenders are creatures of habit – they target familiar areas, learn escape routes and take calculated risks. When reports stack up, the police can track their movements, identify hotspots and deploy resources accordingly. I've personally been part of undercover operations where female officers were sent out as bait to catch serial offenders, but we wouldn't have been there if people hadn't reported incidents first. If the police don't know there's a problem, they can't act on it.

> ### A personal example: Why reporting matters
>
> When I was 17, I worked at a well-known fast-food restaurant. Back in the 1990s, these places weren't open 24 hours, so when I finished late-night shifts at 4am or started early shifts at 5am, I often drove alone to and from work down dark country lanes.
>
> Over time, I noticed an older man, probably in his mid-40s, taking an unusual interest in me. He always chose my queue, even when other queues were shorter, and made strange comments about how pretty I was. At first, I dismissed it – maybe he was just friendly – but my colleagues started teasing me about it, which made me realise how odd it was. Eventually, it escalated. He waited for me outside the restaurant during my early shifts, and one day, he handed me a letter. In it, he described how beautiful I was and how he wanted to take me on holiday, and he also told me to keep it a secret.
>
> At first, I wasn't sure what to do. I felt uncomfortable, but I didn't think it was serious enough to report. Eventually, I mentioned it to my older sister, who immediately told my mum – and that's when things changed. My mum and dad hit the roof and called the police.
>
> A female officer came to my house, read the letter and asked me lots of questions. I felt nervous, sick and guilty, as if I were getting someone into trouble for no reason. Then she told me she needed to speak to my manager. That meant driving to work while a police car followed me, which, at 17, was terrifying

11 - REPORT IT! REPORT IT! REPORT IT!

> – especially since I usually drove like a speed demon. But when I pulled into the car park, he was already there, waiting for me.
>
> I nearly threw up.
>
> I walked straight to the police car and said, "That's him. He's already here waiting for me."
>
> To cut a long story short, he was already known to the police. I wasn't given details at the time, but he was issued a Stalking Prevention Order, which meant that if he came within 100 metres of me, he would be arrested for stalking. Looking back now, I realise that officer knew exactly who he was – I could see it in her face. He was on their radar, and my report helped strengthen their case against him.
>
> These days, we have things like Clare's Law and Sarah's Law, which allow people to check if someone has a history of domestic violence or sexual offences. But even without these tools, one thing remains clear: *if something feels wrong, report it.* You never know what piece of information could stop an offender before they escalate.

Clare's Law

Clare's Law, which is officially known as the Domestic Violence Disclosure Scheme, allows individuals in the UK to request information about a partner's history of abusive behaviour. If you have concerns about someone you're dating or getting involved with, you can contact your local police station or call 101 to make a request. The police will then assess the situation, and if the individual has a history of violence, they may disclose relevant information to help you make an informed decision about your safety.

I highly recommend using this if you have even the slightest suspicion. And if you're unsure about someone, do your own checks too – look at social media, verify their identity and make sure they're not a catfish.

> *When it comes to protecting yourself from potential danger, knowledge is power.*

Sarah's Law

Sarah's Law, which is officially known as the Child Sex Offender Disclosure Scheme, allows parents, carers and guardians in the UK to request information from the police about whether an individual with access to a child has a history of child sexual offences. If such a record exists and disclosing it is deemed necessary for the child's protection, the police will share it with the person best placed to safeguard the child.

This law was introduced following the tragic abduction and murder of eight-year-old Sarah Payne in 2000 by a convicted sex offender. It was designed to empower caregivers with crucial information to ensure they can take the necessary precautions to keep their children safe.

However, police checks are just one layer of protection. It's equally important to do your own research. If you're suspicious about someone, check their social media profiles, verify their identity and look for inconsistencies in their story. Be cautious if they avoid having an online presence altogether or have limited traceable history. If something doesn't feel right, trust your instincts – because when it comes to protecting children, it's always better to be safe than sorry.

CHAPTER 12

Keep an Eye on Each Other

If you've made it this far through the book, you already understand how critical it is to look out for one another. This isn't only about women protecting women; it's about everyone taking responsibility. More than anything, I implore men to pay attention.

I know that, for good men, it can feel frustrating to be viewed with suspicion. But the reality is that you could be a threat, because statistically, so many women are assaulted by people they know: caregivers, family members, partners or friends. Women's wariness isn't paranoia; it's lived experience. And while I'll always encourage women to stay cautious, I also urge men to step up. If you see, hear or suspect a male friend, colleague, family member or stranger is engaging in predatory behaviour, do the right thing.

A few years ago, a 23-year-old guy moved into the flat above me. He seemed nice enough, but something odd happened – my dog growled at him every time he walked down the corridor. This was unusual because my dog had never reacted like that to any other resident. It bothered me, so I asked my partner if we should invite the guy in for a coffee to introduce him to the dog and break the tension.

My partner shrugged and said, "Nah," so I let it go.

A night or two later, while scrolling on the sofa, my partner suddenly shot up, showed me a photo on their phone and asked, "Do we know this guy?"

It took me a moment, but then I recognised him – and more importantly, I recognised the court building in the background. He was a registered sex offender who had been convicted just days before moving into our building.

And how did he get caught?

Because another man – his own friend – had reported him. He'd bragged to his friend about what he'd done! The friend, knowing what the man had done was illegal, had summoned the courage to go to the police. That tip led to investigators securing video evidence of more than one offence being committed by the man in question. Without that report, perhaps he would still be offending.

That friend is a bloody hero. He chose to do the right thing, knowing it would mean turning in someone he knew – and in doing so, he has undoubtedly saved other women from becoming victims.

I'll never let that man into my home, and I'll always trust my dog's instincts. But more than that, I'll always believe that men have a responsibility to hold each other accountable. Predators rely on silence – on people looking the other way, laughing it off or thinking, *That's none of my business.*

But it is your business.

12 – KEEP AN EYE ON EACH OTHER

> *If you hear something, say something. If you see something, report it. If you know someone is a threat, don't stay quiet.*

Because speaking up could save a life.

Keeping-safe tips

Most women, whether they want to or not, have to assess every man as a potential threat. It's not personal; it's survival.

CHAPTER 13

What Can Men Do to Make Women Feel Safer?

I'll say it again: this book isn't an attack on men. There are countless men out there who are kind, respectful and would never dream of harming another person. But if you're a man reading this and wondering what you can do, the reality is that most women, whether they want to or not, have to assess every man as a potential threat. It's not personal; it's *survival*.

Understanding the reality

The physical differences between men and women are significant. Without training, men naturally have about 45% muscle mass, while women have 23%; Even at the lowest estimates, studies consistently show that men have at least 10% more muscle mass than women, not to mention differences in frame size and potential strength.[77,78] This means that being physically overpowered is a real and constant concern for women.

That's why women often cross the street at night when they notice a man behind them. It's not paranoia; it's instinct. And whether you like it or not, this is the reality women live with daily.

So what can you do to help women feel safer? Here are some suggestions:

- **Be mindful of how you move in public spaces**

    If you're walking behind a woman at night, don't silently trail behind her. Instead, cross the street, or if that's not possible, say something like, "Hey, just passing by," in a calm, neutral tone. Yes, she might still feel startled, but at least she'll know your presence isn't a silent threat.

- **Give women space**

    Women often feel physically trapped in tight spaces, whether it's on public transport, in a queue at a bar or walking down the street. Be conscious of how close you stand to women. If you're in a queue, for example, leave space instead of pressing up against them. You might not even notice, but trust me, women do. Far too many women have experienced unwanted physical contact this way.

    Between July 2023 and July 2024 alone, there were 621 reported sexual assaults on women and girls on the London Underground, and that's only the reported cases.[79] That number doesn't include the countless incidents that women simply endure and never speak about.

- **Make yourself look less threatening**

    Simple things can make a difference. If you're wearing a hood up at night, consider taking it down. This isn't about demonising clothing, it's about understanding that a concealed identity can add to a woman's fear. Presenting yourself as non-threatening helps put others at ease.

- **Step up and speak out**

    If you see another man harassing or threatening a woman, do something. That doesn't mean putting yourself in danger, but it does mean not ignoring it. Take action – whether it's calling it out, intervening safely or calling the police – your silence enables the problem. Women are constantly being told to stay vigilant, carry keys between their fingers, avoid dark alleys and never walk alone at night, but the responsibility for change should never be solely on them.

The truth is that women shouldn't have to live in fear just because they exist in public spaces.

Men can play a huge role in making the world feel safer, not by being defensive or dismissive of these issues, but by recognising them and making small, conscious choices to help.

It's not about guilt; it's about *awareness* and *action*.

Keeping-safe tips

Your best defence is awareness, your intuition and your ability to take control of situations before they take control of you.

Conclusion

Awareness, Action and Taking Back Control

Safety isn't just about fear; it's about empowerment. Throughout this book, we've explored practical strategies, real-life experiences and psychological tools to help you become more aware, more prepared and, ultimately, safer. While much of the discussion has focused on male violence against women, it's important to acknowledge that not all perpetrators are men, and not all victims are women. Anyone can be a threat – the same as anyone can fall victim to harm. However, the reality is that, as women, we face disproportionate risks, and this book has been written to equip you with the tools to navigate those risks more effectively.

This isn't about living in constant fear; rather, it's about developing the instincts, habits and knowledge that allow you to move through the world with confidence. It's about recognising the warning signs before danger escalates, knowing how to respond if something feels wrong, and most importantly, trusting yourself and your intuition.

You don't need to be a martial arts expert or carry illegal weapons to stay safe. Your best defence is awareness, your intuition and your ability to take control of situations before they take control of you.

So take what you've learned here and apply it to your life. *Stay alert, trust your gut and look out for others too.* Because true safety isn't only about protecting ourselves; it's about creating a world in which we all stand together, prepared and unafraid.

What follows is a powerful piece that deals with trauma and violation.

Reader discretion is advised.

Between the Cracks

I am not here –
each thrust fractures deep,
unseen by the eye,
but my soul knows.

Tears slip from newly made cracks,
one, two – how many will he carve?
Will the splintered shards ever reach him?
His soul? His skin? His flesh?
Perhaps they might.
Perhaps they should.

But how could this ever be equal?
He uses;
I break.
Flashes of those I once loved creep in –
God, no.
Don't let them become mixed up with him.

I react –
don't react, don't react.
He tells me I enjoy this.
Enjoy the breaking, the tearing.
That's twenty-seven.
Twenty-eight.
Please stop.

BETWEEN THE CRACKS

If there's a God, make him stop.
Undo what I can't.
Thirty-one.
If there's a devil, take him.
For these cracks are deepening,
splitting me into pieces
that will never heal.
Thirty-seven.

The silence now.
Did the devil listen?
The grunting has stopped,
but my body still rocks –
with pain, with rage.

Get off me.
Don't touch me.
Sorry?
Fuck you.

Now, I speak to the devil;
hope he becomes your friend.
But where is my God?
Where are my ancestors?

PREDATOR PROOF

I feel their weeping –
tears falling onto the ruin inside me.
Now it travels out,
leaving me,
but never truly leaving.

The shards remain –
thorns buried deep,
punishing me
with each breath,
each step,
each swallow.

How do I move past this?
How do I live past this?
I am no longer alive,
only trapped in the spaces between –
between the cracks,
between the absence of God,
between the silence of the devil.

Jo Saint 01/02/2025

References

1. Office for National Statistics (2023). *Sexual Offences Victim Characteristics, England and Wales: Year ending March 2022*. Retrieved from: https://www.ons.gov.uk/peoplepopulationandcommunity/crimeandjustice/articles/sexualoffencesvictimcharacteristicsenglandandwales/yearendingmarch2022

2. Office for National Statistics (2023). *Crime in England and Wales: Year ending March 2023*. Retrieved from: https://www.ons.gov.uk/peoplepopulationandcommunity/crimeandjustice/bulletins/crimeinenglandandwales/yearendingmarch2023

3. Wrightbus (n.d.). *NBfL – Build Specification*. [PDF] Retrieved from: https://foi.tfl.gov.uk/FOI-2180-2021/NRM%20-%20Redacted%20Specification.pdf

4. Office for National Statistics (2021). *Nature of Sexual Assault by Rape or Penetration, England and Wales: Year ending March 2020*. Retrieved from: https://www.ons.gov.uk/peoplepopulationandcommunity/crimeandjustice/articles/natureofsexualassaultbyrapeorpenetrationenglandandwales/yearendingmarch2020#understanding-sexual-assault

5. Wrightbus (n.d.). *NBfL – Build Specification*. [PDF] Retrieved from: https://foi.tfl.gov.uk/FOI-2180-2021/NRM%20-%20Redacted%20Specification.pdf

6. Office for National Statistics (2023). *Sexual Offences Victim Characteristics, England and Wales: Year ending March 2022*. Retrieved from: https://www.ons.gov.uk/peoplepopulationandcommunity/crimeandjustice/articles/sexualoffencesvictimcharacteristicsenglandandwales/yearendingmarch2022

7. Office for National Statistics (2023). *Sexual Offences Victim Characteristics, England and Wales: Year ending March 2022*. Retrieved from: https://www.ons.gov.uk/peoplepopulationandcommunity/crimeandjustice/articles/sexualoffencesvictimcharacteristicsenglandandwales/yearendingmarch2022

8. Leicester County Council (n.d.). *Census 2001 Key Statistics: Blaby District – Enderby and St John's Ward*. Retrieved from: https://www.lsr-online.org/files/750/enderby-and-st-johns-ward.pdf

9. City Population (2023). *Enderby*. Retrieved from: https://citypopulation.de/en/uk/eastmidlands/leicestershire/E63002710__enderby/

10. Vision to Learn (2022) *UCLA Study: Impact analysis of Vision to Learn*. Retrieved from: https://visiontolearn.org/impact/ucla-study-impact-analysis-of-vision-to-learn/

11. Thorpe, S., Fize, D., & Marlot, C. (1996). Speed of processing in the human visual system. *Nature, 381*, 520–522. DOI: https://doi.org/10.1038/381520a0

12. Carnes, B. (2010). *Making Learning Stick: 20 easy and effective techniques that transfer training*. Alexandria, VA: ATD Press.

13. Wolfe, J.M., Kluender, K., Levi, D., Bartoshuk, L., Herz, R., Klatzy, R. ...Merfeld, D. (2012). *Sensation & Perception* (4th ed.). Sunderland, MA: Sinauer Associates.

14. Itti, L., & Koch, C. (2001). Computational modelling of visual attention. *Nature reviews. Neuroscience, 2*(3), 194–203. DOI: https://doi.org/10.1038/35058500

15. Zwicky, A.M. (2006). *Why Are We so Illuded?* [PDF] Retrieved from: https://web.stanford.edu/~zwicky/LSA07illude.abst.pdf

16. Purves, D., Augustine, G.J., Fitzpatrick, D., Katz, L.C., LaMantia, A.-S., McNamara, J.O., & Williams, S.M. (2001). *Neuroscience* (2nd ed.). Sunderland, MA: Sinauer Associates.

17. Oakley, D.A. (2004). The reticular activating system and consciousness. *Trends in Cognitive Sciences, 8*(12), 548.

18. MacLeod, C., Mathews, A., & Tata, P. (1986). Attentional bias in emotional disorders. *Journal of Abnormal Psychology, 95*(1), 15–20. DOI: https://doi.org/10.1037/0021-843X.95.1.15

19. Rensink, R.A., O'Regan, J.K., & Clark, J.J. (1997). To see or not to see: The need for attention to perceive changes in scenes. *Psychological Science, 8*(5), 368–373. DOI: 10.1111/j.1467-9280.1997.tb00427.x

20. Strasburger, H., Rentschler, I., & Jüttner, M. (2011). Peripheral vision and pattern recognition: A review. *Journal of Vision, 11*(5), 13. DOI: https://doi.org/10.1167/11.5.13

21. Purves, D., Augustine, G.J., Fitzpatrick, D., Katz, L.C., LaMantia, A.-S., McNamara, J.O., & Williams, S.M. (2001). Visual System, Retina. In *Neuroscience* (2nd ed.). Sunderland, MA: Sinauer Associates.

22. Kolb, H. (2003). How the retina works. *American Scientist, 91*(1), 28–35. Retrieved from: https://www.ncbi.nlm.nih.gov/pmc/articles/PMC1299202/

23. Strasburger, H., Rentschler, I., & Jüttner, M. (2011). Peripheral vision and pattern recognition: A review. *Journal of Vision, 11*(5), Article 13. DOI: 10.1167/11.5.13

24. Purves, D., Augustine, G.J., Fitzpatrick, D., Katz, L.C., LaMantia, A.-S., McNamara, J.O., & Williams, S.M. (2001). *Neuroscience* (2nd ed.). Sunderland, MA: Sinauer Associates.

25. Kolb, H. (2003). How the retina works. *American Scientist, 91*(1), 28–35. Retrieved from: https://www.ncbi.nlm.nih.gov/pmc/articles/PMC1299202/

26. Purves, D., Augustine, G.J., Fitzpatrick, D., Katz, L.C., LaMantia, A.-S., McNamara, J.O., & Williams, S.M. (2001). Visual pathways. In *Neuroscience* (2nd ed.). Sunderland, MA: Sinauer Associates.

27. Purves, D., Augustine, G.J., Fitzpatrick, D., Katz, L.C., LaMantia, A.-S., McNamara, J.O., & Williams, S.M. (2001). Photoreceptors. In *Neuroscience*. (2nd ed.). Sunderland, MA: Sinauer Associates.

28. Cherry, E.C. (1953). Some experiments on the recognition of speech, with one and with two ears. *Journal of the Acoustical Society of America, 25*(5), 975–979. DOI: https://doi.org/10.1121/1.1907229

29. Moruzzi, G., & Magoun, H.W. (1949). Brain stem reticular formation and activation of the EEG. *Electroencephalography and Clinical Neurophysiology, 1*(1–4), 455–473. DOI: 10.1176/jnp.7.2.251

30. Cherry, E.C. (1953). Some experiments on the recognition of speech, with one and with two ears. *Journal of the Acoustical Society of America, 25*(5), 975–979. DOI: https://doi.org/10.1121/1.1907229

31. Moruzzi, G., & Magoun, H.W. (1949). Brain stem reticular formation and activation of the EEG. *Electroencephalography and Clinical Neurophysiology, 1*(1–4), 455–473. DOI: 10.1176/jnp.7.2.251

32. Näätänen, R., & Picton, T.W. (1987). The N1 wave of the human electric and magnetic response to sound: A review and an analysis of the component structure. *Psychophysiology, 24*(4), 375–425. DOI: 10.1111/j.1469-8986.1987.tb00311.x

33. Moore, B.C.J. (2012). *An Introduction to the Psychology of Hearing* (6th ed.). Leiden, Netherlands: Brill.

REFERENCES

34. McDermott, J.H., & Oxenham, A.J. (2008). Music perception, pitch, and the auditory system. *Current Opinion in Neurobiology, 18*(4), 452–463. DOI: https://doi.org/10.1016/j.conb.2008.09.005

35. Rankin, C.H., Abrams, T., Barry, R.J., Bhatnagar, S., Clayton, D.F., Colombo, J., ... Thompson, R.F. (2009). Habituation revisited: An updated and revised description of the behavioral characteristics of habituation. *Neurobiology of Learning and Memory, 92*(2), 135–138. DOI: 10.1016/j.nlm.2008.09.012

36. Goldstein, E.B. (2014). Adaptation and attention. In *Sensation and Perception* (9th ed.). Boston, MA: Cengage Learning.

37. LeDoux, J.E. (1996). *The Emotional Brain: The mysterious underpinnings of emotional life*. New York, NY: Simon & Schuster.

38. Arnal, L.H., Flinker, A., Kleinschmidt, A., Giraud, A.L., & Poeppel, D. (2015). Human screams occupy a privileged niche in the communication soundscape. *Current Biology, 25*(15), 2051–2056. DOI: 10.1016/j.cub.2015.06.043

39. Arnal, L.H., Flinker, A., Kleinschmidt, A., Giraud, A.L., & Poeppel, D. (2015). Human screams occupy a privileged niche in the communication soundscape. *Current Biology, 25*(15), 2051–2056. DOI: 10.1016/j.cub.2015.06.043

40. Edworthy, J., & Hellier, E. (2006). Alarms and human behaviour: Implications for medical alarms. *British Journal of Anaesthesia, 97*(1), 12–17. DOI: 10.1093/bja/ael114

41. Middlebrooks, J.C., & Green, D.M. (1991). Sound localization by human listeners. *Annual Review of Psychology, 42*, 135–159. DOI: 10.1146/annurev.ps.42.020191.001031

42. Heffner, H.E. (1983). Hearing in large and small dogs: Absolute thresholds and size of the tympanic membrane. *Behavioral Neuroscience, 97*(2), 310–318. DOI: 10.1037/0735-7044.97.2.310

43. Heffner, H.E., & Heffner, R.S. (1985). Hearing range of the domestic cat. *Hearing Research, 19*(1), 85–88. DOI: 10.1016/0378-5955(85)90088-6

44. Glendinning, J.I. (1994). Is the bitter rejection response always adaptive? *Physiology & Behavior, 56*(6), 1217–1227. DOI: 10.1016/0031-9384(94)90374-0

45. Behrens, M., & Meyerhof, W. (2009). Mammalian bitter taste perception. *Results and Problems in Cell Differentiation, 47*, 203–220. DOI: 10.1007/400_2008_18

46. Roper, S.D. (2007). Signal transduction and information processing in mammalian taste buds. *Pflügers Archiv – European Journal of Physiology, 454*(5), 759–776. DOI: 10.1007/s00424-007-0247-2

47. Hall, R.L., & Hall, R.A. (1999). Principles of metal toxicology. In *Handbook of Toxicology* (2nd ed.). Boca Raton, FL: CRC Press.

48. Vrij, A. (2008). *Detecting Lies and Deceit: Pitfalls and Opportunities* (2nd ed.). New York, NY: John Wiley & Sons.

49. DePaulo, B.M., Lindsay, J.J., Malone, B.E., Muhlenbruck, L., Charlton, K., & Cooper, H. (2003). Cues to deception. *Psychological Bulletin, 129*(1), 74–118. DOI: 10.1037/0033-2909.129.1.74

50. Navarro, J., & Karlins, M. (2008). *What Every Body Is Saying: An ex-FBI agent's guide to speed-reading people*. New York, NY: William Morrow Paperbacks.

51. Pease, A., & Pease, B. (2004). *The Definitive Book of Body Language*. London, UK: Orion.

52. de Becker, G. (1997). *The Gift of Fear: Survival signals that protect us from violence*. New York, NY: Dell Publishing.

53. Blauer, T. (2006). *Be Your Own Bodyguard*. S.L.: Blauer Spear.

54. Navarro, J., & Karlins, M. (2008). *What Every Body Is Saying: An ex-FBI agent's guide to speed-reading people*. New York, NY: William Morrow Paperbacks.

55. Grayson, B., & Stein, M.I. (1981). Attraction to victim and the criminal attack. *Journal of Social Psychology*, 117(1), 65-71. DOI: 10.1080/00224545.1982.9713407

56. Grayson, B., & Stein, M.I. (1981). Attraction to victim and the criminal attack. *Journal of Social Psychology*, 117(1), 65-71. DOI: 10.1080/00224545.1982.9713407

57. Gigerenzer, G. (2007). *Gut Feelings: The intelligence of the unconscious*. London, UK: Penguin.

58. Gladwell, M. (2005). *Blink: The power of thinking without thinking*. New York, NY: Little, Brown and Company.

59. LeDoux, J.E. (1996). *The Emotional Brain: The mysterious underpinnings of emotional life*. New York, NY: Simon & Schuster.

60. Office for National Statistics (2024). *'I feel like I am living someone else's life': One in seven people a victim of stalking*. Retrieved from: https://www.ons.gov.uk/peoplepopulationandcommunity/crimeandjustice/articles/ifeellikeiamlivingsomeoneelseslifeoneinsevenpeopleavictimofstalking/2024-09-26

61. Wrightbus (n.d.). *NBfL – Build Specification*. [PDF] Retrieved from: https://foi.tfl.gov.uk/FOI-2180-2021/NRM%20-%20Redacted%20Specification.pdf

62. *Protection from Harassment Act 1997*. (1997, 21st Mar). Retrieved from: https://www.legislation.gov.uk/ukpga/1997/40/contents

63. Sheridan, L., & Davies, G. M. (2001). What is stalking? The matching of legal and psychological definitions. *Legal and Criminological Psychology*, 6(1), 3-17. DOI: https://doi.org/10.1348/135532501168204

64. Eurocell (2024). *The Cities Most Affected by Burglaries in the UK*. Retrieved from: https://www.eurocell.co.uk/blog/the-cities-most-affected-by-burglaries

65. Home Office (2023). *Report: Understanding and tackling spiking (accessible)*. Retrieved from: https://www.gov.uk/government/publications/understanding-and-tackling-spiking/report-understanding-and-tackling-spiking-accessible?

66. Anglia Ruskin University (2024). *Study Finds 90% of Drink Spiking Goes Unreported in UK*. Retrieved from: https://www.drinkaware.co.uk/news/90-of-drink-spiking-incidents-go-unreported-according-to-research-by-drinkaware-and-anglia-ruskin-university?

67. Rape Crisis England and Wales (n.d.). *Rape and Sexual Assault Statistics*. Retrieved from: https://rapecrisis.org.uk/get-informed/statistics-sexual-violence/

68. Office for National Statistics (2024). *Domestic Abuse in England and Wales Overview: November 2024*. Retrieved from: https://www.ons.gov.uk/peoplepopulationandcommunity/crimeandjustice/bulletins/domesticabuseinenglandandwalesoverview/november2024

69. Oppenheim, M. (2024, 31 Dec). 'Reality of men's violence': 80 women allegedly killed by men in UK in 2024. *The Independent*. Retrieved from: https://www.independent.co.uk/news/uk/home-news/women-alleged-kills-men-2024-b2672173.html

70. Femicide Census (2025). *2000 Women*. [PDF] Retrieved from: https://www.femicidecensus.org/wp-content/uploads/2025/03/2000-Women-full-report.pdf

71. Long, J., Wertans, E., Harper, K., Brennan, D., Harvey, H., Allen, R., & Elliott, K. (2020). *UK Femicides 2009–2018*. [PDF] Retrieved from: https://www.femicidecensus.org/wp-content/uploads/2020/11/Femicide-Census-10-year-report.pdf

REFERENCES

72. van der Kolk, B. (2014). *The Body Keeps the Score: Brain, mind, and body in the healing of trauma.* New York, NY: Viking.

73. Porges, S. W. (2011). *The Polyvagal Theory: Neurophysiological foundations of emotions, attachment, communication, self-regulation.* New York, NY: W.W. Norton & Company.

74. de Becker, G. (1997). *The Gift of Fear: Survival signals that protect us from violence.* New York, NY: Dell Publishing.

75. Blauer, T. (2006). *Be Your Own Bodyguard.* S.L.: Blauer Spear.

76. van der Kolk, B. (2014). *The Body Keeps the Score: Brain, mind, and body in the healing of trauma.* New York, NY: Viking.

77. Janssen, I., Heymsfield, S.B., Wang, Z., & Ross, R. (2000). Skeletal muscle mass and distribution in 468 men and women aged 18–88 yr. *Journal of Applied Physiology, 89*(1), 81–88. DOI: https://doi.org/10.1152/jappl.2000.89.1.81

78. Miller, A.E.J., MacDougall, J.D., Tarnopolsky, M.A., & Sale, D.G. (1993). Gender differences in strength and muscle fiber characteristics. *European Journal of Applied Physiology, 66*(3), 254–262. DOI: 10.1007/BF00235103

79. Kara, M. (2024, 7 Nov). More action needed to combat sexual offences and harassment on the Tube, say victims. *The Standard.* Retrieved from: https://www.standard.co.uk/news/london/tube-sexual-offences-harassment-victims-safety-measures-london-underground-b1191923.html?

Acknowledgements

I still can't quite believe this is done. To have something out in the world that can help women feel safer and stronger – what a feeling! I'm beyond thrilled.

Apparently, the done thing now is to thank everyone. So here goes...

First, thank you to my publisher Alexa at The Book Refinery and Compass-Publishing UK and to my editor Lindsay at Corten Editorial – who is probably now the safest woman alive after reading this manuscript numerous times. Your support, patience and sharp eyes have made this book better in every way.

To my dad, you'll know after reading this just how much of what I've learned started with you. Thank you for teaching me how to stay aware, strong and safe from a young age. I'm sending you the biggest thanks – and a pub token too (just the one, though, as Mum's watching!).

At home, huge thanks to Batdog, my one-eyed shadow, for tolerating all the delayed walks while I got 'just one more bit' done.

ACKNOWLEDGEMENTS

Sorry, mate, but it's not over yet. The fiction book really is nearly finished (yes, I've been saying that for years). And to my fiancée, thank you for listening to endless book chat and my newest idea; that alone deserves a medal.

Finally, to my brilliant friends and colleagues, thank you for reading, rereading, encouraging and gently reminding me that this work matters. Your belief in this book has helped silence the 'is this good enough?' voice in my head more than you know.

Thank you, truly. And big love.

Jo

About the Author

Jo is a former police officer with frontline experience from years spent responding to crime on the streets of Sussex. Her time in uniform has given her a clear view of the risks women face every day – and how often they're lacking the tools they need to stay safe.

After countless conversations with women who are unsure how to respond to uncomfortable, intimidating or dangerous situations, Jo felt compelled to act. *Predator Proof* is her way of sharing that hard-earned knowledge as practical, honest guidance designed to help women feel more confident, more aware and firmly back in control.

When Jo isn't writing (which, honestly, isn't often), you'll find her walking her one-eyed dog (affectionately known as Batdog), soaking up the outdoors with her fiancée and friends, or enjoying a well-earned pint at the pub – and sometimes the latter two at the same time. Maybe now she can take that well-deserved break and have a holiday!

Printed in Dunstable, United Kingdom